BLESS THIS DESK

BLESS THIS DESK

Prayers 9 to 5

KEN THOMPSON

Abingdon   Nashville

BLESS THIS DESK

PRAYERS 9 TO 5

Copyright © 1976 by Ken D. Thompson

Library of Congress Cataloging in Publication Data
Thompson, Kenneth D   1926-
    Bless this desk.
1. Prayers.   I.   Title.
BV245.T43   242'.2   75-33818

ISBN 0-687-03613-5
Scripture quotations noted JB are from THE JERUSALEM BIBLE, copyright © 1966 by Darton, Longman & Todd, Ltd. and Doubleday & Company, Inc. Used by permission of the publisher.

Scripture quotations noted NEB are from The New English Bible. © the Delegates of the Oxford University Press and the Syndics of the Cambridge University Press 1961, 1970. Reprinted by permission.

Manufactured by the Parthenon Press at Nashville, Tennessee, United States of America

**To Phyl,
my enabler**

FOREWORD

How do we keep in touch with our most real self? How can we see beyond the artificialities of our own culture, beyond the pretense of who we'd like to be, the cover-ups of title or station, the cosmetics of life, within the pain and loneliness, beyond the pinch between fear and ego?

The problem begins early. We fall down and someone says, "Now that didn't hurt, did it?" We are dressed up and sent to a party, and this first brush with society is frighteningly uncomfortable, but we are told, "Now don't forget to say you had a good time." We are hurt by another's thoughtlessness, and when everything in us cries vengeance, a doting parent insists, "Now say you're sorry, and give Uncle Charley a big kiss."

We are taught to hide real emotions, to keep a happy face, to pretend.

We come to church, and the natural boisterousness of youth is shushed, and we're made to feel guilty, "We don't run in God's house." We are seated in a pew, and all about us we see people looking sadly unnatural. We don't know that many of them are victims too. We think maybe it's us, so we try to act like them. We conform to this visible appearance of piety and holiness. We say words with more concern for memorization than meaning, more preoccupied with unison than understanding. We place God on the inferior throne of pretense, and our most real self continues in the lonely hiding of separation which is sin.

In adulthood we bring this separation to bear on other things. We say to ourselves that the God who is so holy that he doesn't like children to run wouldn't be interested in this or that aspect of my business dealings. The One whose house is so big and quiet does not care about the tension and confusion of my office today. The One who wanted me to love when I felt no love doesn't care what my real feelings are toward people who infuriate me, as long as I am civil. The One who expected me to wear only my best clothes, saddest face, and who is locked away in that big building doesn't share my fun and frolic or the things I do when I am away at a convention.

What a breakthrough when we learn he knows us better than we know ourselves! He identifies with our most real self. That is what he loves. What grace when we can rightfully place all things in his hands in a simple, childlike trust.

He is God of all things, and our only charge is to live thankfully.

This book is an attempt to share these thoughts about faith, incarnation, and applied religion with fellow pilgrims.

To that end, I entrust to the reader these most personal experiences which I have called prayers.

K.D.T.

CONTENTS

For the spirit of the Lord fills the whole earth, and that which holds all things together is well aware of what men say.

—Wisdom of Solomon 1:7 NEB

Pigeon Holes, Compartments, and Other Places

It's so separated, Lord,
    this life of work
    and family
    and you.
Just when I'm most involved at work
    and solutions are coming
    and deadlines are being met
    and the race is being won,
    it's time to lay it down—
        dismiss it
        and go home.
But there another life awaits.
    It did not wait while I was gone
    but expects my return.
    A life with people, plans, needs,
    personalities, schedules,
    and a love affair to nurture.
Then it's Sunday and I enter yet the third cell
    to give to you my worship,
    to refresh my soul, to resurrect and to listen,
    to deepen our involvement
        you and me.
But then it's Monday again,
    and it's like putting my hand
    in a familiar glove;
    to pick up work again
    just where it was laid aside
        by tense fingers
        and anxious eyes
        three days ago.

Help me to make just one compartment, Lord,
    out of this trinity of transition:
        work,
        home,
        you.
Must one life be laid down in order for another
    to begin?
O Mystery which is Unity!
Help me, Father, Son, and Holy Spirit!

                                Amen.

Happy those servants whom the master finds awake when he comes. I tell you solemnly, he will put on an apron, sit them down at table and wait on them.
—Luke 12:37 JB

Six-Thirty in the Mourning

I'll never get good at it, Lord,
    this business of getting up
    and going to work.
The sins of the evening
    are visited upon the morning.
    Most days it's just too much.
Today I was late again.
    You know because you heard
    my hurried prayers.
    (I *did* pray, didn't I?)
I drove like a heathen,
    and it didn't seem to matter.
Help me, Lord, to be less concerned
    about the clock
    and more about people
    (including me).
Help me to plan my life better, Lord,
    and to find all the time that's there.
Help me to imagine eternity.
    But when I'm late,
    let there be someone
    who understands as well as you.
Amen.

Late that Sunday evening, when the disciples were to-gether behind locked doors, for fear of the Jews, Jesus came and stood among them. "Peace be with you!" he said, and then showed them his hands and his side.
—John 20:19 NEB

In the Quietness of Conscience

You seem so very close just now, Lord.
    Funny how you seem to come and go.
Yesterday in church you seemed to leave me.
    And then, this morning, just a moment ago,
        you returned.
Must you always come to me through others?
Why is it I can't conjure you up?
I woke up a grouch, Lord,
    but Nancy pretended not to notice.
    She just went about
                things as usual.
Then, as I left the house,
    she said, "I love you."
    And I could hardly stand myself.
Now, as I drive along to work,
    I know that you are here again—
    filling my conscience,
    strengthening my resolves,
    giving a dimension
        to Nancy and me.
O God, how much you know about forgiveness,
    and how much I need to learn
            from you and Nancy.

                                        Amen.

If I lift up my eyes to the hills,
where shall I find help?
Help comes only from the Lord,
maker of heaven and earth.
—Psalm 121:1-2 NEB

Meditation of an Early Bird

Dear Lord, the office is so quiet at this hour.
Arriving early
    has brought a dimension to things
    I seldom see when the tempo picks up.
Now, while it's quiet
    and this whole day lies before me
        unopened and unspoiled,
        help me to remember
        what tranquility is
        (and how it remains
        hidden under shouts
        and bells
        and knocks
        and confusion).
Let me reach back during the day today
    and get the strength I feel right now
    from the knowledge
    that there is peace in your world
        (even when we hide it
        in brief moments
        not at all like these).
                    Amen.

*On their way out they met a man from Cyrene, Simon
by name, and pressed him into service to carry his cross.*
—Matthew 27:32 NEB

I Had to Let Him Go, Lord

Joe just couldn't keep up, don't you see?
I had encouraged him
     and warned him
     (even threatened him).
But even when I was telling him, Lord,
     I knew he couldn't help it.
Who's at fault anyway?
     Personnel, for hiring him?
     Joe, for thinking he could do
     something he couldn't?
     Or me, for firing him?
When you have a job to do
     and your job's a crucifixion
     how do you do it right, Lord?
When will I forget about Joe?
The next time I get a raise?
No, Lord,
     especially not then!

Amen.

During supper, Jesus, well aware that the Father had entrusted everything to him, and that he had come from God and was going back to God, rose from table, laid aside his garments, and taking a towel, tied it round him. Then he poured water into a basin, and began to wash his disciples' feet and to wipe them with the towel.

—John 13: 3-5 NEB

I Agreed to Serve, Lord, but Whom?

Being in business means serving on committees.
It's good for business, Lord,
    and the contacts *are* important.
Like this new thing on which I agreed to lend
    a hand.
    The boss is pleased.
    The committee is pleased.
    And Nancy's proud.
The problem is with me.
When I think about the things
    that really need attention
    and the fact that they don't get
        the same commitment
        (from me or anybody else),
    I'm worried down inside.
Civil rights—literacy—poverty—peace.
    They don't win points
    (and they don't get management's nod).
Why, Lord?
    Why do meet-and-eat groups get
    so much of my life
      while many who are lonely
        have nothing to eat
        and have no committees
        and can't give out points?

Forgive me for looking for the wrong rewards,
    Lord,
and for pretending that what I'm doing is
    important.

O Lord!

*All I can say is this: forgetting what is behind me,
and reaching out for that which lies ahead, I press
towards the goal to win the prize which is God's call
to the life above, in Christ Jesus.*

*Let us then keep to this way of thinking, those of us
who are mature. If there is any point on which you
think differently, this also God will make plain to you.*
—Philippians 3: 14-15 NEB

We Weighed Them, Lord
(Song of the Sales Manager)

Why does it take
     such plotting,
     Lord?
Why can't people
     be self-starters?
Why can't we agree on
     what team effort means?
Must all motivation be a plot?
Must every reward sparkle?
Give us all a greater sense
     of who we are
     and what we can do
     and what we should do.
Forgive the plotters like me, Lord.
     When designing grand schemes
     we sometimes forget
     who keeps the score.

Amen.

Do not store up for yourselves treasure on earth, where it grows rusty and moth-eaten, and thieves break in to steal it. Store up treasure in heaven, where there is no moth and no rust to spoil it, no thieves to break in and steal. For where your treasure is, there will your heart be also.

—Matthew 6:19-21 NEB

They Weighed Me, Lord, and I'm 14 Percent
(Song of the Salesman)

The sales quotas came out today, Lord.
And somebody I never met
    decided what I was worth
    and what I needed to do
    during the next three months
        of my life.
It's impersonal, Lord,
    but then
    contest prizes were announced.
How did they know Nancy wanted a mixer?
There it was, right in front of me.
    Like a dream answered.
    An electrical
    gyrating
    carrot!
Am I so transparent, Lord,
    to a guy at the home office
    I never met?
If I'm slacking off, Lord, let me know.
If this quota requires more than hard work
    let me know that too.
And help me to always go
    after the right prizes.

Amen.

Pilate questioned him again: "Have you nothing to say in your defence? You see how many charges they are bringing against you." But, to Pilate's astonishment, Jesus made no further reply.

—Mark 15:4-5 NEB

Getting Chewed Out
(*The Chewer*)

Why me, Lord?
Why do stinking jobs fall to me?
Somewhere there are persons
    who don't have to fuss at others.
Those who punch a clock
    draw a check
    and do a job
    that's not at all like mine.
Teach me to correct more constructively,
    reprimand more fairly,
    and understand more fully.
Help me, Lord,
    to leave room for you
    in what I say and do
    to yours.

Amen.

"Why, what harm has he done?" Pilate asked; but they shouted all the louder, "Crucify him!"

—Mark 15:14 NEB

Getting Chewed Out
(The Chewee)

Jesus, I got it royally today!
A chewing out by the boss,
    complete with onlookers
    —and no excuse.
Help me now to stop dwelling
    on things I wish I'd said.
And help me not to blame others
    for my own ignorance.
A funny thing happened.
    For a moment today
    —just a flashing moment—
    I remembered your standing accused
    in the judgment hall,
    taking it without a word.
You took it, Lord.
    And you weren't guilty
    like me.
Thanks a lot, Jesus.
    It helped.

Amen.

Nothing therefore can come between us and the love of Christ, even if we are troubled or worried, or being persecuted, or lacking food or clothes, or being threatened or even attacked.

—Romans 8:35 JB

Two Different Worlds: The Himesphere

It's funny how it happens, Lord.
In the midst of busiest days,
    suddenly I see
    the family's picture on my desk.
When I see it (really see it)
    I'm lonely!
Can you imagine?
    Lonely at this noisy office?
I get to thinking that
    I don't know what they're doing.
    And they have no idea
        what I'm doing either.
I wish I was there this very moment.
    To give a kiss.
    To mend a toy.
    To shelter.
    To touch.
    To share.
God, help me to remember how I feel just now
    when I do get home
    and the kids are noisy
    and the grass needs cutting
    and Nancy's worn out.
Help me love more consistently
    the way you do.

Amen.

Almighty God, we entrust all who are dear to us
to thy never-failing care and love,
for this life and the life to come;
knowing that thou art doing for them
better things than we can desire or pray for; through
Jesus Christ our Lord. Amen.
—Book of Common Prayer

Two Different Worlds: The Herisphere

Lord, the house is silent.
Only moments ago
    there was turmoil
    haste
    confusion
    and the clock
        making for hasty words
        shouted reminders
        and sudden good-byes.
Now each to his own duty.
    And mine—
        to tend a house
        sodden now with hush.
How can I tell, Lord,
    what it's like
    to be in school today
    or to sense the tempo
        of my husband's office?
We are all together, Lord,
    in this picture which I dust,
    but each day we fragment a little:
        home
        office
        school.
Help me, Lord,
    in the quiet of this house today,
    to maintain the Spirit of your presence

when day is done
and tempers stretch
and we all have
so much of one another
to renew.

Amen.

But that is not all: there is a great chasm fixed between us; no one from our side who wants to reach you can cross it, and none may pass from your side to us.
—Luke 16:26 NEB

Generation Gaps

Who named it, Lord?
Probably the same giver of names
> who oversimplified things by calling them
> "juvenile delinquency" and
> "cold war" and
> who rediscovered that word, "relevant."

His real name is Charley, Lord.
He's the new boy who's come to work.
> And that "gap" is something personal now:
> It's Charley and I.

It's impatience
> and something I would hope is wisdom.

It's a brash urgency
> and something I like called decorum.

It's a Man and a Boy
> who are more alike
> than either can admit,
> who work together but from
> protected positions:
>> dug-in, defensive.

God, you are both Father and Son,
> without gap of generation:
> in harmony with yourself,
> while in that tension of both
>> change and tradition.

Help us get together, God,
> Charley and me.

Amen.

At his gate, covered with sores, lay a poor man named Lazarus, who would have been glad to satisfy his hunger with the scraps from the rich man's table.

—Luke 16:20 NEB

Hey, I Got a Raise, God!

It was a good day, Lord.
I got all that I had hoped for.
    And I couldn't wait to get home
    with the news.
But then I was listening
    to the car radio—
    they were talking about poverty
    again, Lord.
I want to help others—
    and I give what seems right.
    But I had that raise all spent
    on nobody but me and mine.
How do I manage money, Lord,
    when there are so many places for it
    and it's so hard to get it
    into empty hands
    so far removed?
Your world's gotten so complicated, Lord:
    there's someone somewhere
    that I'd like to give my extra
    fifty bucks to right now.
Help me to care enough
    to find out who that someone is.

                Amen.

What will a man gain by winning the whole world, at the cost of his true self? Or what can he give that will buy that self back?

Profit and Loss Statement

Lord, I pray to find a way
    to add some record
    among the credits and debits
    of this business
of people whose work
    and lives together this year
    underlie these figures
      and exceed the balances struck.
Of newcomers who cast their lot with us,
of retirements and vacations,
of promotions (and the people passed over),
of enthusiasm and patience,
of pulling together.
    But most of all, Lord,
    of people, Lord,
    of people.
    The real product.
    The real gain.
    The real loss.
Lord, let every business
    be for people.

Amen.

"The virgin will conceive and bear a son, and he shall be called Emmanuel," a name which means "God is with us."

—Matthew 1:23 NEB

Printed in U.S.A.

It's Christmas card time again, Lord.
How many thousands we send from our company:
  all neat and restrained,
  worded inoffensively.
We don't mention you by name, Lord,
  (I hope you understand)
  for business isn't supposed
   to do such things.
"Seasons Greetings"
"Happy Holidays"
  who can disagree?
It's a time for thanks
  for business favors,
  for saying warm things
  we were ashamed to say
  all year long when there
  were better opportunities
  than this.
  Can't Christmas allow more than all this?
Peace!
Emmanuel!
Love Incarnate!

  Flat out.
  Plain.
  Certain.
  Right on.

        Amen.

*But at his birthday celebrations the daughter of Herodias
danced before the guests, and Herod was so delighted
that he took an oath to give her anything she cared to
ask. Prompted by her mother, she said, "Give me here
on a dish the head of John the Baptist."*

—Matthew 14:6-8 NEB

Person Power

A representative called on me today, Lord,
    selling a program guaranteed
    to help our people become better.
He was enthusiastic.
Lord, how he was enthusiastic!
    "This releases a whole new person power
    in your business—a positive, sales-minded
    motivation that has been the salvation to
    businesses such as yours across the country!"
I listened and then I looked
    at chapter titles:
    "Making People Like You"
    "Making People Like What You're Selling"
    "Making People Do as You Want Them To"
Do we have these rights, Lord?
    Assuming this man can produce?
    Lord, where does honest effort end
    and manipulation begin?
You have passed it by, Lord,
    all these years since Eden.
You could have made us any way
    but you made us free.
Why, Lord?
    Does your love
    that does not manipulate, dominate, or sub-
      jugate
    mean that I should not buy this plan?
I cannot think we should not develop ourselves.

But Lord, for purposes like these?
O God, who has allowed me
    to fail to love you,
help me to want to love you more
    and to use your children less.

                                    Amen.

*And then you will be innocent and genuine, perfect
children of God among a deceitful and underhand brood,
and you will shine in the world like bright stars because
you are offering it the word of life.*
                    —Philippians 2:14-16 JB

How Do You Get Innocent Again?

I saw it this morning, Lord,
    that unspoiled, open
    innocence of youth.
Clean, honest,
    and naked on the world:
    my son, Lord, my son.
And, for a fleeting moment
    it was me
    (how many years ago?)
    with lines and shadows scrubbed away.
Gone, too, the sophistication
    that so often covers childlike things
        like fear
        and awe
        and love.
God, in your forgiveness,
    give me innocence again,
        just once,
        again.

                    Amen.

God loved the world so much that he gave his only Son, that everyone who has faith in him may not die but have eternal life.

—John 3:16 NEB

Expenses and Excuses

Lord, there's a devil at my elbow
    who whispers to me
    as I complete this
    silly form.
Pink, yellow, and white—
    honesty in triplicate.
An expense account
    is a moment of truth
    with yourself.
Fraud is not the problem,
That's clear and certain
    and is an easy decision.
It's the margin, Lord,
    the fringe
    the self-justifications
        that tempt.
Was the call home really to see
    if there were customer messages
    or just because I wanted
        to hear Nancy's voice
        to warm my heart?
Was the lunch really business?
    Or would I have
    taken Fred out anyway?
It's the marginal things, Lord,
    the times I feel sorry for myself
    and decide that
    my own kind of fairness is best.
What were your expenses, God,
    that I should be made sensitive

in these ways of right and wrong?
A plan postponed?
    A love rejected?
        A cross?
            A Son?
Lord, who will make it up to you?
    —these things that really matter,
    these givings of yourself
    that seem, just now,
            so much more than I could expect?
                                    Amen.

It was not for any fault on the part of creation that it was made unable to attain its purpose, it was made so by God; but creation still retains the hope of being freed, like us, from its slavery to decadence, to enjoy the same freedom and glory as the children of God.

—Romans 8:20-21 JB

Lord, Things Are So Complicated

Unsolvables cry out from every side, Lord.
How can war end when it smolders in our hearts?
How can people be equal, ever, except in your
    sight?
How can machines replace men without a human
    slag pile?
How can your balance of creation be reinstituted?
How can inflation end when spending is a virtual
    thanksgiving
        for having it to spend?
How does it all fit back together, Lord,
        now that we've taken it apart
        and lost the directions
        for reassembly?
You launched it all, Lord,
        in order
        in motion
        in love.
Take it back, Lord.
        Mend.
            Repair.
                Forgive.
And help us know your thinking more,
        that we might help.

Amen.

No man can serve two masters: for either he will hate the one and love the other; or else he will hold to the one, and despise the other. Ye cannot serve God and mammon.

—Matthew 6:24

"No Man Can Serve Two Masters"

Lord, what is *mammon?*
Is it whatever comes first in life?
Struggling for a raise
> working to increase the net
> trying to get a bigger piece of the market
> —are these mammon?
I had thought they were
> the pursuit of happiness and profession.
> The means to provide for loved ones?
No?
Then what is mammon, Lord?
> What is it today?
> Here.
> Where *I* am?
I need to know, Lord,
> for I want to serve the right things
> and in the right way.
Lord, help me to know and understand.

Amen.

The Lord showed favour to Sarah as he had promised,
and made good what he had said about her. She conceived
and bore a son to Abraham for his old age, at the time
which God had appointed.... Abraham was a hundred
years old when his son Isaac was born. Sarah said,
"God has given me good reason to laugh, and everybody
who hears will laugh with me."

—Genesis 21:1-2, 5-6 NEB

In the Middle

It's that time of transition, Lord,
when vocation hits a level plane,
when you can see where it will end,
when your abilities are fully known

> and life's expectancies lessen
> and only your middle keeps growing.

When some of life's goals are reached:
> a house gets paid for,
> a child goes away to school,
> another marries,
> the nest empties,
> and all the children-raising equipment
> gets put away
> > for another generation's use.

It's "middle age," Lord—

> neither coming
> nor going,
> like a lull
> and the lessening of things.

Help me use this time, Lord,

> not as before, with haste;
> not as later, with waste,

but *now*
        with meaning and purpose,
        with excitement.
God, fill it up again
        to full measure!

                            Amen.

I do not even acknowledge my own actions as mine, for what I do is not what I want to do, but what I detest.

—Romans 7:15 NEB

Fragments and Contradictions

Great God! There is such a gap
> between my prayers
> and deeds!
> Between my worship
> and how I really
> act toward you!
Paul said, "That which I would . . .
> and that which I would not."
He knew, Lord,
> how it is.
> He knew.
Help the preacher's words, Lord,
> more nearly fit the needs of my life.
> So that Monday makes sense
>> like Sunday,
> and worship helps me find
>> ways to unite life
>> and be
>> more wholly yours.

Amen.

For (as Scripture says)
  "All mortals are like grass;
  all their splendour like the flower of the field;
  the grass withers, the flower falls;
  but the word of the Lord endures for evermore."
                                    —1 Peter 1:24-25 NEB

Tom Died Last Night, Lord

He died, Lord,
    and a little of me died, too!
Yesterday was business as usual.
The same pressures.
    The same views:
            that life will go on forever
            and the challenge of the moment
            is all there is.
And then it all got totaled up.
    And there's a stillness.
Where are the tensions now, Lord?
What happpened to those things
    that yesterday seemed so urgent?
Help me, Lord, now as I pick up the pieces,
    and clean out Tom's desk,
    to see things
    the way Tom does now.
And help me not to forget too quickly, Lord,
    or fail to remember
    that life is short
    and earnest
    and that you're the timekeeper.
                                    Amen.

But the other kept his distance and would not even raise his eyes to heaven, but beat upon his breast, saying, "O God, have mercy on me, sinner that I am."
—Luke 18:13 NEB

Lord, I Thank Thee That I Am Not

Why, Lord,
   does another's failure
   seem to increase my own security?
A comedian admitted,
   "The poor soul evokes laughter
   because by his ignorance and misery
   we are made aware of our own security."
Why did the Pharisee have to thank you
   that he was not like that poor publican
   standing afar off in the temple?
Life seems like a game
   of one-upmanship sometimes, Lord.
   Survival of the fittest.
Help me not to get puffed up
   when another loses.
Lord, have mercy on me, a sinner.

Amen.

*O God, the Father of our Lord Jesus Christ, our only
Saviour, the Prince of Peace; Give us grace seriously to
lay to heart the great dangers we are in by our unhappy
divisions. Take away all hatred and prejudice, and what-
soever else may hinder us from godly union and con-
cord: that as there is but one Body and one Spirit, and
one hope of our calling, one Lord, one Faith, one Baptism,
one God and Father of us all, so we may be all of one
heart and of one soul, united in one holy bond of truth
and peace, of faith and charity, and may with one mind
and one mouth glorify thee; through Jesus Christ our
Lord. Amen.*

—*Book of Common Prayer*

Integration

They say Barker was hired, Lord,
    just because he's black.
        And it may be.
It seemed natural enough, though,
    to say, "Welcome,"
    and to share a cup of coffee.
I never knew there was prejudice,
    not here, Lord,
    not among my friends.
    Until today.
Wisecracks came slowly at first.
    But then it came:
    "You and that nigger hit it off?"
Publicans and sinners, Lord.
    Guilt by association.
How can it be?
    Not to know what was all around me
    —just beneath a smile?
How can I straddle two worlds
    that seem so very black
    and so very white?
Barker must have sensed it before I did.

Help him to know I tried, Lord,
     honestly tried.
     And help me see the things
     you've left all about me
     to do for you today.

                                        Amen.

Is one of you ill? He should send for the elders of the congregation to pray over him and anoint him with oil in the name of the Lord. The prayer offered in faith will save the sick man, the Lord will raise him from his bed, and any sins he may have committed will be forgiven.
—James 5:14-15 NEB

Sick Call

I saw Walt at the hospital today, Lord.
Not because I had the time
　　or because I had the right words,
but because I thought you'd want me to.
(Wasn't it you I heard in my prayers?)
Well, a couple of us went from the office,
　　and it was uncomfortable.
We joked
　　and teased Walt about laziness
　　pretending sickness
　　chasing nurses
　　taking it easy.
Underneath I wanted to say:
　　"I'm praying for you, Walt.
　　You are my friend.
　　I care."
But it seemed it might sound gushy.
　　And so,
　　we joked and left.
Lord, if I'm going to be useful to you,
　　help me to stop playing it safe.
　　Give me the courage
　　to risk myself for you.

　　　　　　　　　　　　Amen.

O God of peace, who hast taught us that in returning and rest we shall be saved, in quietness and in confidence shall be our strength; By the might of thy Spirit lift us, we pray thee, to thy presence, where we may be still and know that thou art God; through Jesus Christ our Lord. Amen.

—*Book of Common Prayer*

Two Weeks Away from It All!

Lord, what shall I do
    with these days?
Vacation, like heaven,
    is what everybody wants,
but business and my busyness have a death to die.
    A giving up,
    a yielding over.
It's hard, Lord,
    to be part of a machine—
    a part in motion
    grinding away
        and suddenly
        to stop.
Who am I
    when I am not a cog?
What do I do
    when the fever breaks
    and I am alone
        with you
        and I am only me?

        Amen.

If your brother wrongs you, reprove him; and if he repents, forgive him. Even if he wrongs you seven times in a day and comes back to you seven times saying, "I am sorry", you are to forgive him.

—Luke 17:3-4 NEB

Who Deserves Forgiveness?

Joe really screwed things up today, Lord.
He lost a sale
    lost a customer
    and what's worse,
    he ignored our
    usual procedure.
Now I've got to find a way
    to regain the customer
    to save the order
    to change the procedure
    to see it doesn't happen again.
Help me to get this mess cleaned up, Lord,
    and to find a way
    to forgive Joe.
How do you do it, Lord?
    Forgive again and again
    people like Joe
        and me?

Amen.

And when he had sat down with them at table, he took bread and said the blessing; he broke the bread, and offered it to them. Then their eyes were opened, and they recognized him; and he vanished from their sight. They said to one another, "Did we not feel our hearts on fire as he talked with us on the road and explained the scriptures to us?"

—Luke 24:30-32 NEB

There You Were, Lord, in Jack What's-His-Name

You surprised me today, Lord!
When I met Jack for lunch,
    I wasn't thinking much about you.
In fact, I realize now, I had you pegged
    as being back there
    in the suburbs
    where I do all my worshiping
    (and so little of my real living).
Lunch was business,
    but as we ate
    we shared
    deeper concerns.
There it was—words, ideas, hopes, and fears—
    they came pouring out of Jack, Lord,
    and I didn't even know he knew you!
Help me to anticipate your presence
    more often and
    to stop thinking that
    if I'm not in church
    you're not around.

                    Thank you!

Over every building on Mount Zion and on all her places of assembly the Lord will create a cloud of smoke by day and a bright flame of fire by night; for glory shall be spread over all as a covering and a canopy, a shade from the heat by day, a refuge and a shelter from rain and tempest.

—Isaiah 4:5-6 NEB

Caught in the Reign

My God, isn't it raining!
    There was no threat
    when I left for lunch.
But here I stand
    sans coat and umbrella
    huddled in this doorway
    waiting for the chance
    to dash back to the office.
What a peace I feel just now
    in this cease-fire,
    this half-time you have called
    in this day of business battle.

The city pauses.
    That great mass which goes out to lunch
    is now pocketed about
    waiting
    listening
    with thoughts turned inward.
Thank you, Lord,
    for this rain
    this doorway
    this common experience
    shared in the midst of
    an otherwise unsharing day.

Amen.

So they were made to work in gangs with officers set over them, to break their spirit with heavy labour. This is how Pharaoh's store-cities, Pithom and Rameses, were built.

—Exodus 1:11 NEB

Bless Honorable Industry—Nuts!

I'm the world's worst hypocrite, Lord.
Today at the luncheon club
    I got mad at the guy who asked the blessing!
The Council of Churches sent him over.
    (It's their way
    of "serving the business community.")
Who was kidding whom, Lord?
    Did he not understand,
    or did he think you wouldn't?
He said some things about industry
    and fellowship
    and honor.
Is that supposed to change things?
Will that change things?
Isn't there something better for him to do?
And shouldn't we be doing our own praying?
We can't have prayers sprinkled on us, Lord.
    We've got to dredge them up
            before they mean anything.
Forgive us for making a fetish of our meals
        (and a rabbit's foot of our religion).
And teach that young preacher
        the difference between
        "sound and honorable industry"
            and scratching out a living.

Amen.

*Then keep your tongue from evil
and your lips from uttering lies;
turn from evil and do good,
seek peace and pursue it.*

—Psalm 34:13-14 NEB

Bad Breath and Dirty Words

Lord, why is it
    speakers assume
    everybody wants to hear
    their dirty jokes?
It happened again today.
    A qualified man
    had my attention
    when he began.
    My admiration, too.
Then he uncorked a joke
    intended to prove him
    "one of the boys,"
    and I was embarrassed
    for him.
Are such views of sex
    our only real common denominator?
    Is this communication?
My laughter was my embarrassment.
    (But it sounded like approval.)
Help us to communicate on higher levels.
    Give us more to say, Lord,
    and better speakers
    to say it.

                              Amen.

Make no mistake about this: if there is anyone among you who fancies himself wise—wise, I mean, by the standards of this passing age—he must become a fool to gain true wisdom. For the wisdom of this world is folly in God's sight.

—I Corinthians 3:18-19 NEB

The Simple Folk

He stood in my office doorway, Lord,
    hesitant and smiling:
    this pleasant-looking delivery man
    from the sheltered workshop.
The day we agreed to hand assemble
    the rush order to Blake Company,
    I never knew this man
        who closed the gap
      between the possible and the promised.
But now, there he was:
    pieces put together
    schedule met
    promise kept.
He brought more than just the order, Lord,
    this simple man
    who was using so much of all he had.
He smiled at me when I failed to smile.
He took pride in the simple
    (and, I suspect, pity in the profound).
"As a little child," Lord.
    Help me also to put
    the pieces together.

Amen.

*Though I think myself right, his mouth may condemn me;
though I count myself innocent, it may declare me a
hypocrite.
But am I innocent after all? Not even I know that,
and, as for my life, I find it hateful.*
—Job 9:20-21 JB

Crisis-Making

When I said we'd meet the deadline,
  I knew I'd committed us
    to the near impossible.
But it wasn't until
  I started trying to find the ways
  that I realized what that meant.
I feel a need for forgiveness, Lord,
  for the man I asked to work on Sunday
  for the canceled weekend trip home
  for the dinners grown cold
  for the disappointment
    of children I don't know
    (and now never want to meet).
Help me to be more sensitive to the lives of others.
More responsible in my decisions.
More reasonable in my promises.
And somehow, help me get forgiveness
  from those on whom I presume.
  And courage to ask for it more often.
Amen.

Again I tell you this: if two of you agree on earth about any request you have to make, that request will be granted by my heavenly Father. For where two or three have met together in my name, I am there among them.
—Matthew 18:19-20 NEB

Decisions by the Dozen

Twelve of us came, Lord,
    to a meeting for making,
        amid changing circumstances
        and confusion,
            a few decisions,
            just a few.
And for the hour a dozen positions remained:
    lines drawn,
    personalities asserted,
    and listening
    overwhelmed by speaking.
How can so many
    made so differently
    find agreement
        in business matters
    or, for that matter,
        concerning you?
But then,
    you chose a dozen
    and they, too,
        were different men.
Help me to find
    among the dilemma of differences in life
    a purpose for all
    that still leaves room
        for doubt and difference

(but not betrayal).
In the end, Lord,
    let us witness our common need
    for you
    and for one another.

                                Amen.

You know (do you not?) that at the sports all the runners run the race, though only one wins the prize. Like them, run to win! But every athlete goes into strict training. They do it to win a fading wreath; we, a wreath that never fades.

—I Corinthians 9:24-25 NEB

He's a Company Man

Jim's a "company man," Lord,
    but he's taking a terrible beating.
    He looks good.
    He makes the right wake.
    He's there at the right time.
    (And with the right people.)
    But he's got the wrong things up front
        it seems.
And, he's worried, Lord.
    I can sense it.
    And I'm too far removed to help.
His wife shows the strain.
    His kids kick up a fuss.
    His supply of pills is increasing.
He's burning out, Lord,
    and for all the wrong reasons.
Help Jim slow down, Lord,
    for his own good
    and everyone else's.
Help him try to please others less
    and you more.
And keep me from being so blamed pious
    when I'm no better programmed than Jim.

Amen.

I Beat Him Down, Lord, and Myself Too!

Maybe you don't know
>about the insides of the inside, Lord.

Business is a lot of things.
>And one is getting the best price, whatever way.

>Nobody says it's our policy
>>but everybody knows it works that way.

Today I guess I did well
>by company standards.

>But the pressure I put on that guy
>has left me under pressure, too.

I could have liked him.
>(He was mighty decent up to a point.)

>But now, I guess he'll dread calling on me
>>the way I dread
>>>calling on Old Man Thornton.

I was thinking, Lord,
>about a cartoon I once saw.

>The boss chewed the employee.

>The employee fussed at his wife.

>The wife scolded the kid.

>And the kid kicked the dog.

I guess I started some ripples in the pool today,
>and now I wish I had done it differently.

I hate the system.
>And most of all, just now,
>I don't like myself.

>>>>>>Amen.

During supper Jesus took bread, and having said the blessing he broke it and gave it to the disciples with the words: "Take this and eat; this is my body."
—Matthew 26:26 NEB

Coffee Breaks Aren't Long Enough

It happens every time, Lord.
>Just as the guys open up
>to what seems worthwhile talking about
>somebody says,
>>"Well, we gotta get back at it."
And there are left
>empty cups
>wadded napkins
>cigarette butts
>and those unexplored thoughts,
>>half-expressed aspirations,
>>moments of possible communion
>>that people sometimes share.
Lord, help us to do more thinking
>and not be satisfied with
>old clichés
>old prejudices
>old habits
>and old defenses.
You who made the table holy,
>be Lord of the coffee break, too.

Amen.

*But Moses said, "O Lord, I have never been a man of
ready speech, never in my life, not even now that thou
hast spoken to me; I am slow and hesitant of speech."
The Lord said to him, "Who is it that gives man speech?
Who makes him dumb or deaf? Who makes him clear-
sighted or blind? Is it not I, the Lord? Go now; I will
help your speech and tell you what to say."*

—Exodus 4:10-12 NEB

It's a Sales Call I've Been Putting Off

God, I need to talk with you this moment
    before I get out of the car.
This call is going to be hard.
    Mr. Thornton's impossible to please.
    I always hate myself for trying.
I'll have a long wait as usual.
    They say it's Thornton's way
    of softening you up.
Then he'll give me a hard time
    for the last delivery being late.
    And he'll use it to beat my price down.
I need the business, God, and yet
    I need my self-respect, too.
Help me to remain who I am and still do the job.
Help me to keep the account, God,
    and somehow, help me
    find a way to like this man
    who helps feed my kids.

                                Amen.

"What will you give me to betray him to you?" They
weighed him out thirty silver pieces.

—Matthew 26:15 NEB

Somebody's Going to Get Stuck

They say, God, that our old standard
    Model 17 HL
    isn't showing the profit it should.
    (Still, its popularity is holding well.)
The fellows in the plant
    say they can reduce the special machining
    and use a lighter metal for the frame,
    adding thirty percent more profit for us!
Now, that's well and good.
    (Those guys are trained for such as this.)
But who should speak for the customers, Lord?
    They're going to get less and pay the same.
It doesn't seem right
    but it does seem like good business!
Thirty percent
    or thirty pieces of silver?

Amen.

I give you a new commandment: love one another; as I have loved you, so you are to love one another. If there is this love among you, then all will know that you are my disciples.

—John 13:34-35 NEB

Mr. Whitaker Went to Pasture Today

Old man Whitaker retired today, God.
    Got the watch,
    kind words,
    and center of attention.
I kidded him
    about sleeping late
    and playing golf all the time
    (while I continue slaving).
But I know he's going to be lost
    with nothing to do.
    (Was my happiness really
    because it wasn't happening to me?)
I hope Whit stays useful to himself, Lord.
    And that he doesn't get too tired
    of sleeping late
    and playing golf
    and taking walks.
Help us find ways to keep in touch
    —and better ways than gold watches
    to say "I love you" to one another.
                    Amen.

Better the end of anything than its beginning; better patience than pride.

Your World Is Made of Paper, God

Dear God! What's happening to us?
The new procedure was issued today.
    It took the whole morning
    and my lunch hour
    to sort through it.
Two things stand out:
    there'll be more paper work than ever
    and more training for Harry and Walt.
How can I implement all this, Lord?
    Harry's already got more than he can do.
    Walt's three procedures are behind time now.
    Both are too old for change, Lord,
    and too young to retire.
Help me, God, through boring tasks
    and forms in triplicate.
And, God, help Harry and Walt, too.

                        Amen.

*David and Abishai entered the camp at night and found
Saul lying asleep within the lines with his spear thrust
into the ground by his head. Abner and the army were
lying all round him. Abishai said to David, "God has put
your enemy into your power today; let me strike him
and pin him to the ground with one thrust of the spear;
I shall not have to strike twice." David said to him, "Do
him no harm; who has ever lifted a finger against the
Lord's anointed and gone unpunished? As the Lord lives,"
went on David, "the Lord will strike him down; either his
time will come and he will die, or he will go down to
battle and meet his end. God forbid that I should lift
a finger against the Lord's anointed! But now let us
take the spear which is by his head, and the water-jar,
and go."*

—I Samuel 26:7-11 NEB

Unfair Competition

I guess you know the spot I was in
    this morning, God.
The boys in sales came up with an idea
    to "knock competition out of the ring."
Barney said it might even break 'em.
(I must admit, it should work.)
While I didn't say so,
    I'll admit to you
    I don't know whether I really
    want to "break 'em" or not.
Does business always have to be
    at somebody's expense or failure?
What insipid piety, Lord!
    I don't gripe on payday!
How do I see a thing like this?
    When I'm paid to compete,
    and I know there's another guy
    competing too
    —and you're on both sides!

Help me to speak up
        and still not be a fool.
And, God, help me to make sense
        to you
        and to myself,
        a hypocrite.

Amen.

God blessed the seventh day and made it holy, because on that day he ceased from all the work he had set himself to do.

—Genesis 2:3 NEB

Fingerprints on Creation

The project got bigger, Lord.
Everyone had his finger in it.
It started so simply:
    a good idea
    lying bare and fresh
Problem = solution.
    So beautiful
    and unencumbered.
But a committee got the project,
    and it's become bogged down
    in that frozen state
    of suspended life
    of analysis
    of research
    of indecision.
Where did it go, that fresh, new thought?
Who erased my fingerprints?
What has happened
    to that simple, unspoiled,
    uncommitted portion of creation?
Your world is like that,
    isn't it, Lord?
When your handprint was so clear
    your intention so simple
    your love so evident?
God, help us find the simpler ways.
    Search the unfathomable love that
    kept it so simple as
    "the evening and the morning
        were the first day."

(64)

Like manger beds
        and wooden crosses
        and a new creation
        that needs to be
                loved into existence.

                                Amen.

For everything its season, and for every activity under heaven its time:

    a time to be born and a time to die;
    a time to plant and a time to uproot;
    a time to kill and a time to heal;
    a time to pull down and a time to build up;
    a time to weep and a time to laugh;
    a time for mourning and a time for dancing;
    a time to scatter stones and a time to gather them;
    a time to embrace and a time to refrain from embracing;
    a time to seek and a time to lose;
    a time to keep and a time to throw away;
    a time to tear and a time to mend;
    a time for silence and a time for speech;
    a time to love and a time to hate;
    a time for war and a time for peace.
                 —Ecclesiastes 3:1-8 NEB

Deadlines Are Killing Me

Back in Palestine, Jesus,
    I guess nobody had to meet deadlines.
Now everybody's in a rush.
"If I wanted it tomorrow,
    I'd have asked for it tomorrow."
    That's the slogan.
    Every week needs two Fridays.
    Every month an extra week.
I meet most of them, Jesus,
    but it causes me to
    treat people in ways I don't like.
    (And it causes me to treat myself
    in a way that's killing, too.)
Mary and Joseph were meeting deadlines, though,
    weren't they?
    The time to be taxed.
    The time to give you birth.
    —"The fullness of time . . . ."
They did it.

And in a stable!
Jesus, help me to get a better perspective
of time
and priorities
and your coming again.

Amen.

*So the Word became flesh; he came to dwell among us,
and we saw his glory, such glory as befits the Father's
only Son, full of grace and truth.*

—John 1:14 NEB

Communicating and Communing

I'm sending another
    head-office memo.
And suddenly I'm aware
    that the task is not so much
    to give understanding as
    to simply get others to
    act the way the system requires.
There's no two-way communication intended, Lord.
No chance for reason
    or for someone down the line
    to have that great need
    for personal understanding met
    by the therapy of conversation.
"Effective Immediately!" it reads.
But you know
    commandments don't work,
    do they, Lord?
It took a lot to communicate, didn't it?
    A Son
        a cross
            an empty tomb.
Help me to watch for better ways
    than memos and directives.
Help me to share more
    and dictate less.

Amen.

Teach us to order our days rightly,
   that we may enter the gate of wisdom.
   How long, O Lord?
Relent, and take pity on thy servants.
Satisfy us with thy love when morning breaks,
that we may sing for joy and be glad all our days.
Repay us days of gladness for our days of suffering,
for the years thou hast humbled us.
                         —Psalm 90:12-15 NEB

Surely You Didn't Make Fridays, Lord!

We're told creation
      was all done
      in orderliness
      with forethought
      and in love.
And so, we've set ourselves
      a calendar.
Sunday isn't really first, Lord.
      It all starts with Monday.
      It's the day of business
      and not feeling up to things.
The middle of the week brings some hope
      because then you've almost recovered from
         Monday
            and you haven't endured Friday.
Then Friday comes.
      (And somebody's made a mistake, Lord.)
      You've only got as many hours in Friday
         as in the other days!
      And it doesn't work well at all.
Saturday's we're justified to loaf.
      (Justified by what happens the other days.)
Then Sunday comes (yes, last of all),
      and somehow perspective returns.
But it's followed by Monday
      and that's a prelude to Friday again.

Help us reapportion things, Lord,
    so that days get equalized
    and each is more like Sunday.
And help me, too, to remember that you once took
    a Friday
    and made it Good.

                                    Amen.

Father, if it be thy will, take this cup away from me.
—Luke 22:42 NEB

Before a Meeting on Friday
(The Final Flinch)

God, I dread the next two hours!
Ever since they set the date
    I've dreaded it.
    Because it's the kind of meeting
    that drags on forever.
I don't have anything to offer.
    But most of all, God,
    I suspect no one has
    anything to give me, either.
Got my smokes
    my mints
    my yellow pad for doodling—
    but still I'm not looking
        forward to it.
Help me to sense the needs of the man
    who called this thing together.
    And help me to listen.
No time is really lost
    if people are together
    (even past five o'clock Friday)
    learning one another.

                  Amen.

He came back and found them asleep; and he said to Peter, "Asleep, Simon? Were you not able to stay awake for one hour? Stay awake, all of you; and pray that you may be spared the test. The spirit is willing, but the flesh is weak."

—Mark 14:37-39 NEB

Working Overtime's a Drag, Lord

Right up until quitting time
    it looked like I'd be on my way
        home
        family
        rest.
But then came that last order!
    Lord, the whole day
    seemed turned upside down!
The phone calls home gave excuse.
    Replies were the same:
    hurt and
    disappointment.
When you want to do one thing, Lord,
    and life requires another,
    who's at fault?
Give me a second wind
    and help me do my best
    anyhow.
What is the order, Lord?
Family? Job? Church? Play? You?
How can I keep it all in perspective?
Lord, help me!

                        Amen.

When he came in sight of the city, he wept over it.
—Luke 19:41 NEB

He Beheld the City and Wept Over It

Lord, I know why you cried.
>The city. Nitty gritty. Pity.
How calloused I have made myself
>not to see
>the misery that this city holds.
Look straight ahead
>over the dashboard's chrome and colored
>>lights
>bound for work and then for home
>listening to a stereo tape
>over the quiet hum of the air conditioner
>in sterile
>>sealed
>>>seclusion.
Keep them at the curb, Lord,
>I cannot stand to see
>the people who really live down here,
>who watch me come and go
>getting what they cannot get
>>from this city.
And, leaving them behind each night
>upon this scorched field of commerce.
>Dirty gutters.
>Noise of traffic.
>Cloud of fumes.
>Empty boxes.
>Darkened buildings.
The city people, window washers, and sweepers
>come out of hiding
>like forest animals when the hunter leaves.
God, give me the courage to see forthrightly
>all that is really here,

(73)

especially this slag pile of picked-over people,
that my guilt and the chamber of commerce
tell me is not here.
Teach me to clean up
the messes I have made.
Cause me to care.
Lord, help me to bear the pain of caring
for these people I have refused to see.
The ones I desert every night
and leave for you to comfort.

Amen.

O God, whose fatherly care reacheth to the uttermost parts of the earth; We humbly beseech thee graciously to behold and bless those whom we love, now absent from us. Defend them from all dangers of soul and body; and grant that both they and we, drawing nearer to thee, may be bound together by thy love in the communion of thy Holy Spirit, and in the fellowship of thy saints; through Jesus Christ our Lord. Amen.

—*Book of Common Prayer*

Grounded

(*Socked in with Your Thoughts*)

This is a miserable airport, God.
I've done all I can in this strange town
    and it looks like
    I'll never get a flight out.
Now all I want is to get back home tonight
    and be with the family.
Am I different?
    Does everybody get homesick like me?
Nancy and the kids
    seem worlds away just now, Lord.
    They are at home, going about things as
      usual.
    It's just that I'm 600 lousy miles away
      and there's nothing I can do about it.
They're sitting down to supper about now.
Help me to be with them somehow.
Stay with me tonight, Lord,
    and with them, too.

                    Amen.

Then Jesus gave a loud cry and said, "Father, into thy hands I commit my spirit."

—Luke 23:46 NEB

God Has No Hands but My Hands

God, what a flight!
The weather's rotten
 and this plane's got me
  at my wit's end.
Into the hands of what kind of man
 have I placed my life this night?
This pilot, whom I do not know
 and right now
 trust so little.
Is he on his way home, too?
Is there someone expecting him,
 this man I've never seen,
 this technician
  who preserves and delivers?
How do you stand it, Lord?
 to have to put your work
 in the hands of others
  that they might find
  that fragile line between
  their will and yours
  and choose each day?
Lord, give me the confidence in this pilot
 that you have shown
 in both of us.

       Amen.

Walt Disney's

The Sorcerer's Apprentice

Adapted by
Don Ferguson

Illustrated by
Peter Emslie

A GOLDEN BOOK • NEW YORK

Golden Books Publishing Company, Inc., Racine, Wisconsin 53404

*L*ong, long ago, there lived a powerful sorcerer who had a young apprentice named Mickey.

Every day the little apprentice swept the floors, polished the sorcerer's crystal ball, and carried water from the well to the sorcerer's magic pool.

Late one afternoon a bat was fluttering around the sorcerer's head. As Mickey watched, the sorcerer raised his arms and said, "MUTATIS!" The bat magically turned into a beautiful butterfly.

But the trick had tired the old sorcerer.
He yawned and put his sorcerer's hat down
upon his table. Then he slowly walked up
the stone steps to his bedchamber.

Mickey was alone in the sorcerer's workshop.

Mickey couldn't take his eyes off the sorcerer's hat.

He crept to the sorcerer's workbench, held the mysterious hat in his hands—and then placed it on his head.

At that moment Mickey felt full of magic.

Mickey looked around the workshop. There against the wall stood his old broom. As he had seen his master do, Mickey raised his arms and said, "Mutatis!"

The broom began to glow.

At Mickey's command, the broom's handle
sprouted arms—and its straw divided into two legs!
The broom had come to life! But would it obey
the commands of a young apprentice?
"Pick up the buckets!" Mickey said.
The broom obeyed.

Mickey led the broom to the well.
"Fill the buckets here!" Mickey ordered the
broom. Once again the broom obeyed.

Carrying the two buckets of water, the broom
followed the little apprentice back to the sorcerer's
magic pool.

"Empty the buckets here!" Mickey told the
broom. "Then do it all over again!"

Back and forth went the broom, from the well to the pool.

Feeling very pleased with himself, Mickey climbed up into the sorcerer's chair to relax while the broom did his work.

It wasn't long before the little apprentice was asleep—and dreaming.

Mickey dreamed that he was the most powerful sorcerer in the universe. At his command, the stars danced and the planets whirled through the sky!

Far below the mountaintop, the oceans raged
and roared at Mickey's command.

Higher and higher the waves crashed until
Mickey felt the cold, wet spray of the water . . .

SPLASH!
This was no dream. The magic pool was overflowing. The enchanted broom had done Mickey's work all too well!

"Stop!" shouted Mickey.

The broom did not stop. It marched right over Mickey, dumped more water into the pool, and went back to the well.

"Mutatis!" cried Mickey. But the broom did not obey. It filled its buckets instead.

Frantic, Mickey snatched an ax from the wall and waited for the broom to return with its brimming buckets. Then he raised his arms and *chop—chop—chopped* the broom into a thousand splinters!

All was silent—for a moment.

Suddenly each splinter jumped off the floor, sprouted arms and legs—and became a broom. And each broom carried two buckets!

The army of brooms with its hundreds of buckets marched from the well to the pool and back again. The water was getting deeper . . . and deeper.

By now the little apprentice was swimming for his life. How he struggled to stay afloat! When the sorcerer's book of spells floated by, Mickey climbed on top of it.

Turning the pages as best he could, he looked desperately for a spell that would stop the enchanted brooms.

Suddenly the book began to spin. Mickey was caught in a whirlpool!

He felt himself being pulled down, down . . . down!

The last thing Mickey heard as he went under
was the thundering voice of the sorcerer.

"MUTANDIS!" boomed the sorcerer from the
top of the stone steps.

Instantly the water vanished and the army of
marching brooms was no more.

The sorcerer's apprentice knew he was in a lot of
trouble. With a gulp, Mickey returned the magical
hat to the sorcerer.

Making a hasty exit, the sorcerer's apprentice
felt himself being swooshed out of the room.
    "Don't forget your broom!" said the sorcerer.
    And if Mickey had looked, he would have seen
the sorcerer smiling.